OFF WITH THE OLD, ON WITH THE NEW

A Biblical Guide to Cultivating Character in Your Children

Stephanie Ripple

To Ian and Adrianna, the guinea pigs of this process

"I have no greater joy than this, to hear of
my children walking in the truth"
—3 John 1:4

CONTENTS

*Though this is provided for your convenience, I highly recommend you look up the Scripture passages in your Bible.

INTRODUCTION

Many excellent books have been written on the topic of Christian parenting. I know this because I read stacks of them as we raised our kids. As useful as those books were, I never found what I was truly looking for. I longed for a resource that would not only help me systematically *disciple* my children and cultivate godly character but also be a quick reference guide in moments when *discipline* was called for.

Since no such book existed, I began to write it myself. Back then it was not the tidy volume you hold in your hands right now; it consisted of piles of laminated cardstock bound in the corner by book rings. Despite the imperfections, that pile of papers helped my husband and me accomplish all that we prayed for and more. As I used it in tandem with God's Word and prayer, I witnessed the transformation of our kids' hearts. I watched them learn to seek the Lord to help them lay aside the old self and clothe themselves in the new. As Hebrews 12:11 declares, "All discipline for the moment seems not to be joyful, but sorrowful; yet to those who have been trained by it, afterwards it yields the peaceful fruit of righteousness." Using this process for discipline often was not joyful for any of us in the moment, but many people who visited our home commented on the sense of peace they experienced there.

I marvel now as I observe my kids. My oldest is mature beyond his years, married, and raising two little ones of his own, and my youngest has grown into a delightful teenager, actively pursuing her childhood dreams. Though they aren't perfect, they exhibit humble confidence in who the Lord has created them to be. Their lives overflow with Holy Spirit fruit. I give God all the glory for this—His Word and His Spirit have accomplished these things in their lives.

I cannot promise you these exact results, but I can reiterate the truth that God's Word will never return empty. His Word *will* accomplish what He desires in the lives of your children (Isaiah 55:11).

Instructions
for Parents

> Fathers [and mothers], do not provoke your children
> to anger, but bring them up in the discipline and
> instruction of the Lord. —Ephesians 6:4

L iving with a houseful of perfectly behaved children sounds like a beautiful thing, doesn't it? Many may envy such a life, but be careful, Mom and Dad. Consider Jesus's reproof in Matthew 23:25–28 (emphasis mine):

> "Woe to you, scribes and Pharisees, hypocrites! For you clean the outside of the cup and of the dish, but inside they are full of robbery and self-indulgence. You blind Pharisee, *first* clean the inside of the cup and of the dish, so that the outside of it may become clean also.

> "Woe to you, scribes and Pharisees, hypocrites! For you are like whitewashed tombs which on the outside appear beautiful, but inside they are full of dead men's bones and all uncleanness. So you, too, outwardly appear righteous to men, but inwardly you are full of hypocrisy and lawlessness."

You certainly do not want to be bringing up a bunch of little Pharisees! Avoid this by making a habit of teaching your children to address the heart, the inner man, *first*, and expect more honorable behavior to follow. Sanctification is a lifelong process; don't demand perfection from your kids. When they fall short, lead them to the cross of Christ, where He paid the penalty for their sin (Romans 3:23–25). Pray that His extravagant kindness will lead them to repentance (Romans 2:4). Commit to the challenge of walking alongside them as they work out their salvation with fear and trembling (Philippians 2:12).

When they do well, continue to point them to Christ. Teach them to deflect praise when appropriate and to give Him all the glory (Psalm 115:1). Praise Him for the peace and joy that characterize your home as you all learn to follow Him more closely (Romans 15:13). Allow your children to witness your commitment to and pursuit of Christ. They are much more apt to listen to your instruction if it aligns with the pattern of your own life.

You will likely feel inadequate along this child-rearing journey at times. Each new age and stage will present unique challenges, but remember that God has chosen you to raise these particular children. He has provided everything you need to bring them up in the discipline and instruction of the Lord and to instill godly character in them.

I have heard some parents assert, "It is not wise to use Scripture as discipline because it will put a bad taste in children's mouths for the Bible." Moms and Dads, you are believing a lie and not God if this is your reasoning! A quick study of 2 Timothy 3:16–17 tells us otherwise:[1]

All Scripture is . . .

inspired by God, *divinely inspired (DBY), breathed out by God (ESV), given by inspiration of God (NKJV), God-breathed (YLT)*
and
profitable, *beneficial (NASB), useful (NIV),*
for
teaching, *doctrine (NKJV), to teach us what is true (NLT)*
(In Greek, meaning "instruction, that we might be taught, for our learning")

---

[1] In bold here is the NASB1995 translation, and then in italics are various translation renderings, and below some of the words and phrases you will find depth of meaning according to the Greek definitions of these words.

for
reproof, *conviction (DBY), rebuking (NIV), to make us realize what is wrong in our lives (NLT)*
(In Greek, meaning, "for convicting one of his sinfulness")
for
correction, *correcting (NIV), it corrects us when we are wrong (NLT)*
(In Greek, meaning, "restoration to an upright or a right state; improvement of life and character")
for
training, *instruction (NKJV), teaches us (NLT)*
(In Greek, meaning, "instruction which aims at the increase of virtue")
in
righteousness, *what is right (NLT)*
(In Greek, meaning, "integrity, virtue, purity of life, uprightness, correctness in thinking, feeling, and acting")
so that the
man of God, *servant of God (NIV), His people (NLT),*
(In Greek, meaning, "man devoted to the service of God, God's minister")
may be
adequate, *complete (ESV), fully capable (NASB)*
(In Greek, meaning, "complete, perfect, special aptitude for given uses")
equipped, *fitted to (DBY), thoroughly equipped (NIV)*
(In Greek, meaning, "to furnish perfectly")
for every
good work.
(In Greek, meaning, "good work springing from piety")

Off with the Old, On with the New is not meant to be an exhaustive resource. The hearts of you children are deep waters. Seek God for wisdom to draw them out. Allow Him to lead you to Scripture passages that will be the most transformative for each of them. May using this resource alongside God's Word and prayer make the path a bit clearer and more joyful for you and your family!

Getting Started

- Purchase a special journal and pen for each child.
- Purchase a set of sticky tabs to mark the following sections (optional, but so helpful!):
  - Instructions for Parents
  - Instructions for Children
  - Character Qualities
  - Quick-Reference Scripture Guide
  - Character Quality Definitions

Using This Resource

Family Discussion

- Choose one character quality pair to focus on each week. Discuss the definition of both the new-self and the old-self character qualities.
- Encourage your children to think of biblical characters who display each of the qualities.
- Invite your children to think of a friend or family member who displays the new-self quality and discuss specific examples of when and how that quality was displayed.
- Have each family member share how well they think they themselves demonstrate the new-self quality and whether or not they struggle with the old-self quality.

Independent Study

- Read through the "Instructions for Children" with your child the first time they do these independent study tasks. I highly encourage you to walk through this process with them the first few times or until they become comfortable doing it on their own. Each week in their journal for the qualities you are currently studying, have them look up and write out the definitions for both the old-self and the new-self qualities under the "Gain Understanding" heading.
- Have your child read through the questions under the "Examine" heading. You may require them to answer one or more in writing, allow them to do this part in their hearts and minds, or have them discuss the answers with you.
- Have your child look up the verses under the "Be Transformed" heading. You may require them to write out one or more of the verses, read them aloud, or simply read them silently.
- Have your child say or write the prayer under the "Pray" heading. Encourage them to personalize the prayer by adding their own words.
- Make sure your child knows they can come to you for help along the way.

Discipline

- Decide whether your child will receive immediate consequences when displaying old-self character qualities or if you will give a warning first. During a time of peace, discuss this with your child so they know what to expect when discipline is necessary.
- When your child exhibits an old-self quality, have him or her work through the independent study process outlined above for the character quality with which he or she is struggling.

- Determine and discuss ahead of time whether each step will be approached through discussion, writing, or silently in the child's heart and mind. Make sure your child is aware of exactly what will be required of him or her before disciplinary action is needed.
- Be consistent!

Focused Character Transformation

- At the beginning of a new year or a new school year, help each other (this includes you, too, Mom and Dad) determine two to three areas of character struggle. Encourage each family member to confess at least one area for which they know they fall short. Invite one another to gently and kindly point out blind spots that need to be worked on. Guide your children to speak the truth in a loving way without name calling. For example, "I notice you struggle to tell the truth when you think you may get in trouble for it," rather than, "You are a liar!".
- Have each family member choose Scripture passages to memorize that correspond with his or her own areas of struggle.
- Invite one another to accountability in laying aside the old self and putting on the new self. Allow your kids to address respectfully when you are operating from the old self.

**Note: You will find the Table of Contents and the Character Qualities segments ordered alphabetically by the new-self character qualities. The Quick-Reference Scripture Guide is alphabetized according to the old-self character qualities. This will allow you to quickly find what you are looking for if you happen to forget which character qualities pair together.

Instructions
for Children

> Hear, O sons, the instruction of a father [and mother], and give attention that you may gain understanding, for I give you sound teaching; do not abandon my instruction. —Proverbs 4:1–2

Before I give instruction to you children, it is vital that you understand that your salvation is a free gift from God, not a result of your good works or good behavior (Ephesians 2:8–9)! Your righteous deeds on their own are like filthy rags (Isaiah 64:6). You need the righteousness that comes through faith in Christ to be counted worthy before God (Romans 1:17). God will not love you more if you behave in a godly way, and He will not love you less if you behave in an ungodly way. Christ demonstrates His love for you in that while you were yet a sinner, He died for you (Romans 5:8). Why bother to do all this work if it doesn't earn you favor with God? Because God gets glory when you grow (2 Peter 3:18)! Plus, your life and the lives of those around you will be most satisfying when you are doing what you were created to do: give God glory (Isaiah 43:7).

Follow the steps below for each character quality, and you will become a doer of God's Word as described in Ephesians 4:22–24: "In reference to your former manner of life, you lay aside the old self, which is being corrupted in accordance with the lusts of deceit, and that you be renewed in the spirit of your mind, and put on the new self, which in the likeness of God has been created in righteousness and holiness of the truth."

1. Gain Understanding

How blessed is the man who finds wisdom and the man who gains understanding.
—Proverbs 3:13

How can you know what is expected of you if you don't know the meanings of the old-self and new-self qualities your parents want you to learn about? **Take a moment to read the definitions of the old-self and new-self qualities you are studying or working on.**

2. Examine

> *Let us examine and probe our ways,*
> *and let us return to the LORD.*
> —Lamentations 3:40

Jesus often asked questions to help people examine their hearts and minds in order to come to a deeper understanding of themselves and why they behave the way they do. **Take a moment to answer some probing questions and examine your ways with regard to the quality you are studying or working on.**

3. Be Transformed

> *And do not be conformed to this world, but be transformed by*
> *the renewing of your mind, so that you may prove what the will*
> *of God is, that which is good and acceptable and perfect.*
> —Romans 12:2

God's Word is living and active and has the power to transform you. Just as your physical body grows when you eat bread, so you grow spiritually when you nourish yourself with the words of the Bread of Life. **Look up and meditate on the suggested verses. Consider digging for some of your own.**

4. Pray

> *My help comes from the LORD, who*
> *made heaven and earth.*
> —Psalm 121:2

Apart from Christ you can do nothing. He is the One who will transform you. He is faithful to answer when you call. **Say or write out the prayer. Add some words of your own if you like.**

Enjoy the adventure of following Christ and becoming the person God created you to be!

CHARACTER QUALITIES

1

ALERTNESS
vs.
Unawareness

Being aware of that
which is taking place around me
so I can have the right response to it

*Keep watching and praying that you may not come into
temptation; the spirit is willing, but the flesh is weak.*
—Mark 14:38

Gain Understanding

Lay Aside—Unawareness
Put On—Alertness

Examine

1. How can alertness help me avoid danger?
2. How can unawareness cause me to miss opportunities?
3. What causes me to be unaware, and what can I do to change that?

Be Transformed

Mark 14:38
1 Corinthians 16:13
1 Thessalonians 5:6
1 Peter 5:8

Pray

Lord Jesus, You were never ignorant about what was going on around You. You were perfectly and completely aware of both the physical and spiritual realms. I confess that I sometimes have the wrong responses to people and situations or no response at all because I fail to be on the alert. Thank You for the dangers and opportunities you make me aware of when I am alert. Please help me to remain aware at all times.

2

ATTENTIVENESS
vs.
Unconcern

Showing the worth of a person
by giving him undivided attention
and showing respect and courtesy

*Do nothing from selfishness or empty conceit, but with humility of mind
regard one another as more important than yourselves; do not merely look
out for your own personal interests, but also for the interests of others.*
—Philippians 2:3–4

Gain Understanding

Lay Aside—Unconcern
Put On—Attentiveness

Examine

1. What does lack of concern for others reveal about my heart?
2. What were, and are, Jesus's interactions with people like?
3. In what ways can I give my full attention to others?

Be Transformed

Luke 6:31
Romans 12:10
Philippians 2:3–4

Pray

Lord, every time I come to You, You give me Your undivided attention and are interested in what I have to say. Thank You. Forgive me for regarding myself as more important than others and showing no interest in their thoughts, ideas, and words. Help me to think of others above myself so that I can honor them and give my full attention to them.

3

AVAILABILITY
vs.
Self-Centeredness

Making my own schedule and priorities
secondary to the wishes
of God and those I am serving

For I have no one else of kindred spirit who will genuinely
be concerned for your welfare. For they all seek after
their own interests, not those of Christ Jesus.
—Philippians 2:20–21

Gain Understanding

Lay Aside—Self-centeredness
Put On—Availability

Examine

1. Whom do I belong to and why? What is my response to this truth?
2. How is God asking me to make myself available for the good of others?
3. How will I worship God by offering myself for the sake of others?
4. Whom am I living for?

Be Transformed

Isaiah 6:8
Romans 12:1
1 Corinthians 6:20
2 Corinthians 5:15
Philippians 2:20–21

Pray

I confess I am often concerned only with my own needs, desires, and interests instead of considering the needs and desires of others. Jesus, You were so quick to make Yourself available! When people sought You when You went off alone to pray, You made Yourself available to them. When You were on Your way to care for an urgent need and someone else needed You along the way, You made Yourself available. I am Yours. Help me to live for You and those You've put in my life.

4

BOLDNESS
vs.
Fearfulness

Willingness to venture out and do
the right thing at the right time
regardless of obstacles or fears I may face

*And now, Lord, take note of their threats, and grant that Your
bond-servants may speak Your word with all confidence.*
—Acts 4:29

Gain Understanding

Lay Aside—Fearfulness
Put On—Boldness

Examine

1. What do I know to be true about God that can give me boldness and courage?
2. What is the best way to deal with a fearful situation?
3. Is anything or anyone more powerful than God? How can knowing the answer to this question ease my fears?
4. What kind of spirit has God given me? What kind of spirit has He not given me?

Be Transformed

Deuteronomy 31:6
Proverbs 29:25
Matthew 8:26
Acts 4:29
2 Timothy 1:7

Pray

Lord Jesus, while You were here, You boldly stood for what is true and right and good, knowing the danger it put You in. Forgive me when I am too fearful to do the same. Thank You that You have not given me a spirit of timidity. Please grant me boldness!

5

CAUTION
vs.
Haste

Knowing how important
right timing is
in accomplishing right actions

Also it is not good for a person to be without knowledge,
and he who hurries his footsteps errs.
—Proverbs 19:2

Gain Understanding

Lay Aside—Haste
Put On—Caution

Examine

1. Have I erred because I was speaking or acting hastily? How could things have turned out differently if I had chosen to think before I spoke or acted?
2. Do I plan ahead and count the cost when making big decisions?
3. What end can I expect if I continue to speak and act in haste?

Be Transformed

Proverbs 19:2
Proverbs 21:5
Proverbs 29:20
Luke 14:28
James 1:19

Pray

Lord, Your thoughts and ways are so much higher than mine, and You are good to those who wait for You. I confess that I frequently run hastily ahead of You and do things my own way. Thank You that Your timing is always perfect, even when it's hard for me to understand. Please help me to practice cautiousness by carefully considering what the results of my words and actions might be.

6

COMPASSION
vs.
Indifference

Conveying deep love and concern
and meeting the needs of those
facing struggles and distress

Bear one another's burdens, and thereby fulfill the law of Christ.
—Galatians 6:2

Gain Understanding

Lay Aside—Indifference
Put On—Compassion

Examine

1. Why does God comfort me and show me compassion when I am in distress? What can I learn from this? What action can I take?
2. What does it say about my heart when I am indifferent to the suffering of others?
3. How should I treat a friend who is suffering?

Be Transformed

Job 6:14
2 Corinthians 1:3–4
Galatians 6:2
1 John 3:17

Pray

Lord, as a father has compassion for his children, so You have compassion on those who fear You. Please forgive me for being indifferent to those You have put in my path who are struggling and in distress, for refusing to bear their burdens. Help me to see people through Your eyes of compassion. Thank You for the many ways You comfort me when I am suffering. Teach me how to share that comfort with others.

7

CONTENTMENT
vs.
Covetousness

Realizing that in Christ
I have all I need

*Not that I speak from want, for I have learned to be content
in whatever circumstances I am. I know how to get along with
humble means, and I also know how to live in prosperity; in any
and every circumstance I have learned the secret of being filled and
going hungry, both of having abundance and suffering need.*
—Philippians 4:11–12

Gain Understanding

Lay Aside—Covetousness
Put On—Contentment

Examine

1. According to God's Word, what do I need to be content?
2. Will more stuff truly make me happy? What do I truly need that I don't have?
3. Do I rejoice in the things that money can't buy more than temporal possessions?

Be Transformed

Exodus 20:17
Luke 12:15
Philippians 4:11–12
1 Timothy 6:8
Hebrews 13:5
1 John 2:15

Pray

Forgive me, Lord, for being discontented and desiring that which You have not given me. Please free me from the love of the things of this world. I have never gone hungry, I have never been without shelter or clothing, and You have never left my side. There is nothing else I truly need to be happy. Please give me faith to believe this.

8

CREATIVITY
vs.
Underachievement

Being resourceful and imaginative
in using the best of the goods and talents
I have to serve the Lord

God created man in His own image, in the image of God
He created him; male and female He created them.
—Genesis 1:27

Gain Understanding

Lay Aside—Underachievement
Put On—Creativity

Examine

1. How can observing God's creation inspire me to be creative myself?
2. Instead of sulking and complaining of boredom, how can I use the gifts, skills, and talents God has given me at this moment?
3. What new ideas can I come up with to make life better for myself and others?

Be Transformed

Genesis 1:27
Proverbs 22:29
Ephesians 2:10
Colossians 3:23
1 Peter 4:10

Pray

God, You are the Creator of this amazing universe, and You have created me in Your image! I am Your workmanship, and I know You have special plans for me. Thank You for the unique gifts and talents You have given me. I confess I sometimes fail to use them to my full potential. Help me to use my imagination to fully apply myself to serve You and others.

9

DECISIVENESS
vs.
Double-Mindedness

The ability to finalize difficult decisions
based on accurate facts, wise counsel,
and clear direction from God's Word

*But if any of you lacks wisdom, let him ask of God, who gives to all
generously and without reproach, and it will be given to him.*
—James 1:5

Gain Understanding

Lay Aside—Double-mindedness
Put On—Decisiveness

Examine

1. How can I discover what the will of God is when making a decision?
2. Can I completely trust God to guide me and give me wisdom?
3. Do I seek wise counsel before making decisions?
4. What causes me to doubt?

Be Transformed

Proverbs 19:20
Romans 12:2
2 Corinthians 10:5
James 1:5
James 1:6–8

Pray

God, You are the source of all wisdom. I confess I sometimes I forget to seek You when making decisions and sometimes I don't trust You to guide me. Thank You for your generous promise to give wisdom whenever I ask. Help me to take my thoughts captive to the obedience of Christ, to be free from doubt, and to confidently go forward with decisions You've helped me make.

10

DEFERENCE
vs.
Rudeness

Limiting my freedom in order
not to offend the tastes of those
whom God has called me to serve

*It is good not to eat meat or to drink wine, or to do
anything by which your brother stumbles.*
—Romans 14:21

Gain Understanding

Lay Aside—Rudeness
Put On—Deference

Examine

1. Am I participating in activities that many other Christians believe are wrong?
2. Am I stubbornly unwilling to yield to the tastes and preferences of those around me?
3. Am I doing anything that may lead someone else in my life to sin?
4. To whom can I show preference and honor?

Be Transformed

Romans 12:10
Romans 14:21
1 Corinthians 8:9
1 Corinthians 8:13

Pray

Lord Jesus, You put the needs and desires of others above your own when You walked on this earth. Forgive me for failing to show concern for the feelings of others and rudely demanding my own way. Teach me to limit my freedom when exercising it may be harmful to a brother or sister. May I never be a stumbling block to another. Help me to show preference to others.

11

DETERMINATION
vs.
Discouragement

Purposing to accomplish
God's goals in God's time
regardless of the opposition

*Let us not lose heart in doing good, for in due time
we will reap if we do not grow weary.*
—Galatians 6:9

Gain Understanding

Lay Aside—Discouragement
Put On—Determination

Examine

1. Where am I finding my strength?
2. What is the benefit of not giving up?
3. When things were really difficult, did Jesus give up? How did He handle difficulties?

Be Transformed

Matthew 26:38–39
Galatians 6:9
Philippians 4:13
2 Thessalonians 3:13
Hebrews 12:3

Pray

Jesus, Your determination to carry out Your Father's will to sacrifice Your life so that I might have eternal life is amazing. You did this all the while knowing the pain and suffering You would face. Thank You for not allowing Yourself to be overcome by discouragement. I confess I sometimes get discouraged and want to give up. Please strengthen me for the for the work You have prepared for me so that I do not grow weary and lose heart.

12

DILIGENCE
vs.
Laziness

Regarding each task
as a special assignment from the Lord
and using all my energies to accomplish it

*Whatever you do, do your work heartily, as for the Lord rather
than for men, knowing that from the Lord you will receive the
reward of the inheritance. It is the Lord Christ whom you serve.*
—Colossians 3:23–24

Gain Understanding

Lay Aside—Laziness
Put On—Diligence

Examine

1. What are some consequences of laziness? Rewards of diligence?
2. Whom am I truly working for? How can that energize me to do the work?
3. What happens to my relationship with God and with others when I refuse to do my best work?

Be Transformed

Proverbs 12:24
Proverbs 13:4
Ephesians 2:10
Colossians 3:23–24
Hebrews 6:10–12

Pray

Lord Jesus, You were never lazy. You found so much satisfaction in carrying out the will of Your Father and accomplishing the work He gave You. Forgive me for my lack of effort. Thank You for the work You have prepared for me and created me to do. Help me always to work heartily and remember that it is You whom I serve.

13

DISCERNMENT
vs.
Judgment

The God-given ability
to recognize the difference between
truth and error, between good and evil

*But the LORD said to Samuel, "Do not look at his appearance
or at the height of his stature, because I have rejected him;
for God sees not as man sees, for man looks at the outward
appearance, but the LORD looks at the heart."*
—1 Samuel 16:7

Gain Understanding

Lay Aside—Judgment
Put On—Discernment

Examine

1. Am I making a rash judgment about someone's salvation or the motivation of their heart?
2. Am I looking at outward appearances alone, or have I sought God in His Word and prayer for discernment?
3. Is there sin in my life that might be distorting my understanding?

Be Transformed

1 Samuel 16:7
Luke 6:41–42
Hebrews 5:13–14

Pray

God, You alone are the judge of all the earth. You clearly see our thoughts and the depths of our hearts. Forgive me for thinking I can sit on Your throne and rashly judge the thoughts and intentions of others! Thank You for offering me the meat of Your Word. Make me quick to draw near to You in prayer and confession and train my senses to discern good and evil.

14

DISCRETION
vs.
Carelessness

The ability to avoid words, actions,
and attitudes that could result
in undesirable consequences

*The prudent sees the evil and hides himself, but
the naive go on, and are punished for it.*
—Proverbs 22:3

Gain Understanding

Lay Aside—Carelessness
Put On—Discretion

Examine

1. What are the results of being careless? For myself? For others?
2. What should I do when I recognize the potential for an undesirable consequence because of my words, actions, or attitudes?
3. Do my words really matter to God?

Be Transformed

Proverbs 11:13
Proverbs 13:3
Proverbs 14:16
Proverbs 20:19
Proverbs 22:3
Matthew 12:36–37

Pray

So often, God, I forget to think before I speak and act! Every word You speak and every action You take is good and right and pure. Teach me to guard my mouth so no careless words escape. Help me to think before I act so I don't walk right into trouble.

15

EDIFYING
vs.
Tearing Down

Choosing gracious words
that bless, build up,
and encourage others

*Let no unwholesome word proceed from your mouth, but only
such a word as is good for edification according to the need of
the moment, so that it will give grace to those who hear.*
—Ephesians 4:29

Gain Understanding

Lay Aside—Tearing Down
Put On—Edifying

Examine

1. Are my words encouraging, a blessing to those around me, or are they discouraging and critical?
2. According to God, is it okay to say critical or discouraging words and then say I was joking?
3. How can I use the gifts God has given me to build up those in the church?

Be Transformed

Proverbs 26:18–19
Ephesians 4:8, 11–12
Ephesians 4:29
1 Thessalonians 5:11

Pray

Though we deserve condemnation, You have shown us mercy, given us words of life, and You sing and rejoice over us! Forgive me for being critical, judgmental, and condemning toward those whom You have created in Your image. Thank You for the gifts You have given those in Your body, the church, that we might build one another up. Help me to speak only gracious words that bless, encourage, and edify.

16

ENTHUSIASM
vs.
Apathy

Being positive, optimistic, and zealous
even when I experience
setbacks or disappointments

*Looking for the blessed hope and the appearing of the glory of
our great God and Savior, Christ Jesus, who gave Himself for us
to redeem us from every lawless deed, and to purify for Himself
a people for His own possession, zealous for good deeds.*
—Titus 2:13–14

Gain Understanding

Lay Aside—Apathy
Put On—Enthusiasm

Examine

1. What should my energy and attitude be as I serve the Lord and others?
2. According to God's Word, is it possible to show enthusiasm even when I'm sorrowful?
3. What am I enthusiastic about? Is that consistent with how God desires me to live?

Be Transformed

Romans 12:11
2 Corinthians 6:10
Philippians 4:4
1 Thessalonians 5:16
Titus 2:13–14

Pray

Lord, You are zealous to be glorified, and rightly so. Forgive me for my apathy. Help me to have joy even when sorrowful things happen in my life. Make me passionate about the things that are important to You. Jesus, remind me often that You will one day make a glorious return to this earth. As I wait for that day, make me zealous for every good deed You have prepared for me to do.

17

FAITH
vs.
Unbelief

Confidence that actions rooted in
God's Word will yield the best outcome
even when I can't see how

Now faith is the assurance of things hoped for,
the conviction of things not seen.
—Hebrews 11:1

Gain Understanding

Lay Aside—Unbelief
Put On—Faith

Examine

1. Am I focusing my eyes on that which I can see or that which is unseen? How is that affecting my faith?
2. Where does my faith come from?
3. How can I exercise my faith and have less unbelief?
4. What power does faith give me?

Be Transformed

Mark 9:24
Romans 12:3
2 Corinthians 4:18
2 Corinthians 5:7
Ephesians 6:16
Hebrews 11:1

Pray

God, You have shown Yourself to be faithful and true. Forgive my unbelief! Grow my faith in You and Your Word. Help me to believe You even when it doesn't seem to make sense. Help me to keep my eyes fixed on eternal things. Teach me to protect myself from the lies of the enemy by using the shield of faith. Thank You for the measure of faith You have given me.

18

FAITHFULNESS
vs.
Inconsistency

Fulfilling my commitments
to God and others even if
it means unexpected sacrifice

*In whose eyes a reprobate is despised, but who honors those who
fear the LORD; He swears to his own hurt and does not change.*
—Psalm 15:4

Gain Understanding

Lay Aside—Inconsistency
Put On—Faithfulness

Examine

1. Can people count on me to follow through with what I say I will do?
2. Am I failing to be faithful because I am thinking of myself before God and others?
3. If a task becomes difficult, do I make excuses not to finish?
4. What blessings can I expect as a result of faithfulness? Do I really want to miss out on these things?

Be Transformed

Numbers 30:2
Psalm 15:4
Matthew 25:23
Revelation 2:10

Pray

Lord, You are always faithful. We can always count on You to keep Your promises. Thank You for the great sacrifices You have made to keep Your word. I confess there are so many ways I fail to be faithful. Sometimes I forget to do the things I've promised. Sometimes I'm too selfish to make the sacrifices faithfulness requires. Lord, help me to be the kind of person who can be counted upon.

19

FLEXIBILITY
vs.
Resistance

Not setting my affections
on ideas or plans that could be
changed by God or others

Set your mind on the things above, not on the things that are on earth.
—Colossians 3:2

Gain Understanding

Lay Aside—Resistance
Put On—Flexibility

Examine

1. What does it say about my heart if I am unwilling to allow my plans to be changed?
2. What kinds of things does God say I should be setting my mind on and pursuing?
3. How can having an eternal perspective help me remain flexible?
4. When plans are changed, do I get discouraged, or do I trust God to bring good from the new plans?
5. Who is ultimately in charge of my plans?

Be Transformed

Psalm 145:17
Colossians 3:2
2 Timothy 2:3–4
James 4:13–15

Pray

You are sovereign, God. Why do I ever think I am in control and try to exert my will on others? Keep my heart and mind focused heavenward so that when plans change, I will not become upset. All Your plans and purposes are right and good. Thank You that You are kind in all Your deeds. May Your will be done.

20

FORGIVENESS
vs.
Bitterness

Clearing the record of those
who have wronged me and allowing God
to love them through me

*Be kind to one another, tender-hearted, forgiving each
other, just as God in Christ also has forgiven you.*
—Ephesians 4:32

Gain Understanding

Lay Aside—Bitterness
Put On—Forgiveness

Examine

1. Why should I forgive in my heart even if a person who hurt me hasn't sought my forgiveness?
2. How does God say I should repay evil done to me?
3. What if someone continues to commit the same sin against me over and over?
4. When someone sins against me, should I completely overlook it? What is the proper response?

Be Transformed

Matthew 18:15–16
Matthew 18:21–22
Romans 12:21
Ephesians 4:32
Colossians 3:13
1 Peter 3:9

Pray

Jesus, You forgave the men who nailed You to the cross while You were still hanging there! Through Your blood shed on that cross, You have forgiven all my sins. Thank You for such a priceless gift. Help me neither to reject those who have wronged me nor to grow bitter. Help me to offer forgiveness as freely as You do and even bless those who wrong me.

21

GENEROSITY
vs.
Stinginess

Realizing that all I have
belongs to God and using it
for His purposes

Now this I say, he who sows sparingly will also reap sparingly,
and he who sows bountifully will also reap bountifully.
—2 Corinthians 9:6

Gain Understanding

Lay Aside—Stinginess
Put On—Generosity

Examine

1. Does stinginess benefit me in any way?
2. What are the rewards of generosity?
3. What kind of attitude does God expect me to have when I share the things He has given me?
4. Who truly owns all that I call mine?

Be Transformed

Psalms 24:1
Proverbs 11:24–25
Matthew 7:9–11
2 Corinthians 9:6–7

Pray

You don't give us stones when we ask for bread. No, You give us good gifts far beyond anything we ask or imagine. Forgive me for stingily hoarding the gifts You have given me. Help me to have open hands and to share generously and cheerfully.

22

GENTLENESS
vs.
Harshness

Showing personal care,
tenderness, and the love
of Christ toward others

But we proved to be gentle among you, as a nursing
mother tenderly cares for her own children.
—1 Thessalonians 2:7

Gain Understanding

Lay Aside—Harshness
Put On—Gentleness

Examine

1. How do people typically react to gentleness? To harshness?
2. What blessings can come from resisting the temptation to be harsh and being gentle instead?
3. How can I be as gentle as a mother is with her baby to those in my life?

Be Transformed

Proverbs 15:1
Matthew 5:5
Philippians 4:5
1 Thessalonians 2:7

Pray

God, Elijah looked for You in the strong wind, in the earthquake, and in the fire, yet he heard Your voice in a gentle whisper. Thank You for being like a shepherd with his sheep, so full of gentleness. Forgive me for being harsh in my thoughts, words, and deeds. Please grow the fruit of gentleness in me.

23

HONESTY
vs.
Deception

Accurately reporting
past facts, present observations,
and future intentions

Therefore, laying aside falsehood, SPEAK TRUTH EACH ONE *of you*
WITH HIS NEIGHBOR, *for we are members of one another.*
—Ephesians 4:25

Gain Understanding

Lay Aside—Deception
Put On—Honesty

Examine

1. Whose example am I following when I choose to be deceitful?
2. How does deception affect my relationships with my friends and family? With God?
3. Do I take deception and lying as seriously as God does?
4. What do I learn in the Word about how God views deception and lying?

Be Transformed

Proverbs 6:16–17
Proverbs 12:22
Mark 7:21–22
John 8:44
Ephesians 4:25

Pray

Jesus, You are the Way, the *Truth*, and the Life, and it is impossible for You to lie. Thank You that Your words are always true! You hate lying and list it in Your Word alongside such a despicable sin as the shedding of innocent blood. I confess I have been deceptive. Buckle the belt of truth around my waist and make me an honest person.

24

HOSPITALITY
vs.
Aloofness

Cheerfully sharing food, shelter,
spiritual refreshment, and myself
with those whom God brings into my life

Be hospitable to one another without complaint.
—1 Peter 4:9

Gain Understanding

Lay Aside—Aloofness
Put On—Hospitality

Examine

1. Who has given me all that I have? Am I lacking anything?
2. What should my response be to such generosity?
3. Whom has God asked me to show hospitality toward?
4. How can I show hospitality toward Jesus?

Be Transformed

Matthew 25:35–40
Romans 12:13
Hebrews 13:2
1 Peter 4:9

Pray

Lord, forgive me for my lack of excitement to share my things and myself. Thank You for coming into this world and fully sharing Yourself and all You have with us. I know I should be practicing hospitality without complaint when You present the opportunity. Remind me that as I serve others, You count it as serving You. Grow this desire in me.

25

HUMILITY
vs.
Pride

Recognizing that my achievements
result from the investments
of others in my life

*But He gives a greater grace. Therefore it says, "God is opposed
to the proud, but gives grace to the humble."*
—James 4:6

Gain Understanding

Lay Aside—Pride
Put On—Humility

Examine

1. How does God respond to humility? To pride?
2. Do my words and actions bring glory and honor to God or myself?
3. When people disagree with me, do I argue for my position?
4. Do I have trouble admitting when I am wrong? Am I quick to correct others when they are wrong?
5. Is it ever okay to boast?

Be Transformed

Proverbs 25:27
Proverbs 27:2
Luke 14:11
2 Corinthians 10:18
James 4:6

Pray

I confess I have been seeking my own glory! Jesus, even though You are God, You did not regard equality with God a thing to be grasped, but emptied Yourself and became a man so that You might die to save prideful sinners. Help me to remember that I can do nothing, nor would I have anything, apart from You. Teach me to humble myself so that You might exalt me.

26

INTEGRITY
vs.
Hypocrisy

Being as genuine on the inside
as I appear to be on the outside

*Woe to you, scribes and Pharisees, hypocrites! For you
are like whitewashed tombs which on the outside appear
beautiful, but inside they are full of dead men's bones and all
uncleanness. So you, too, outwardly appear righteous to men,
but inwardly you are full of hypocrisy and lawlessness.*
—Matthew 23:27–28

Gain Understanding

Lay Aside—Hypocrisy
Put On—Integrity

Examine

1. Does the life that people see on the outside match who I am on the inside? Are there secret sins in my heart that I am hiding from the light of Christ?
2. Am I tolerating hypocrisy in those around me? What danger does this present?
3. What benefits come along with integrity?
4. How can regularly confessing my sins guard me from becoming hypocritical?

Be Transformed

Proverbs 11:3
Matthew 23:27–28
2 Corinthians 1:12
Galatians 2:13
1 John 1:9

Pray

Jesus, You are the same yesterday, today, and forever. You never try to pretend You are someone You are not. You are perfect, yet You do not look down upon or condemn me for being imperfect. Forgive me for trying to appear more righteous than I am and for looking down on others who are caught in sin. Instead, make me quick to confess my own sin and to show grace and forgiveness to others. Thank You that You are faithful to cleanse me of all unrighteousness. Make me a person of integrity.

27

JOY
vs.
Self-Pity

Expressing delight in my relationship
with Christ, His creation, others, and my circumstances
as I live in harmony with the Lord and others

You will make known to me the path of life; in Your presence is
fullness of joy; in Your right hand there are pleasures forever.
—Psalm 16:11

Gain Understanding

Lay Aside—Self-pity
Put On—Joy

Examine

1. Where is true joy found?
2. When should I have joy?
3. In what can I find joy when circumstances in my life feel difficult?
4. How can I fight for joy when I am tempted to feel sorry for myself?

Be Transformed

Psalm 16:11
Psalm 21:6
John 3:29
James 1:2
1 Peter 1:3–6

Pray

Lord, You have caused Your Spirit to dwell in me, You speak to me through Your Word, You stand with me through trials, You have given me faith and saved me, and You have an imperishable inheritance waiting for me in heaven. I have so much to rejoice in! Forgive me for feeling sorry for myself and help me to find joy in Your presence.

28

KINDNESS
vs.
Cruelty

Doing good to others from the heart
in thought, word, and deed

*But love your enemies, and do good, and lend, expecting nothing in
return; and your reward will be great, and you will be sons of the
Most High; for He Himself is kind to ungrateful and evil men.*
—Luke 6:35

Gain Understanding

Lay Aside—Cruelty
Put On—Kindness

Examine

1. Am I delighting in someone else's pain, distress, trouble, or adversity? How should I treat other people?
2. How does being kind affect me? Being cruel?
3. To whom does God ask me to be kind?
4. Should I expect anything in return for showing kindness?

Be Transformed

Proverbs 3:3
Proverbs 11:17
Matthew 7:12
Luke 6:35

Pray

Father, You have shown the riches of Your kindness to me in Jesus. You are kind even to ungrateful and evil men. You have asked me to show kindness even to my enemies, yet I find myself being cruel even to my family at times. Please forgive me and grow the fruit of kindness in me.

29

LOVE
vs.
Selfishness

Caring for others
without having personal reward
as my motive

And if I give all my possessions to feed the poor, and if I surrender
my body to be burned, but do not have love, it profits me nothing.
—1 Corinthians 13:3

Gain Understanding

Lay Aside—Selfishness
Put On—Love

Examine

1. Are my actions showing greater love for myself or for others?
2. Is there any eternal reward in doing good deeds that are not motivated by love?
3. How can I follow Jesus's example of love?
4. What is the source of my love?

Be Transformed

John 15:13
1 Corinthians 13:3
1 Corinthians 13:4–7
1 John 3:16
1 John 4:19

Pray

Jesus, I know the only reason I have the capability to love is because You first loved me. And You loved me in the greatest way possible by laying down Your life for me! Thank You for such extravagant love. I confess I often think only of myself. Please cleanse the selfishness from my heart and help me to love freely without expecting anything in return.

30

OBEDIENCE
vs.
Self-Indulgence

Listening to the voice of,
submitting to the will of,
and following Christ

*Now those who belong to Christ Jesus have crucified the flesh with its
passions and desires. If we live by the Spirit, let us also walk by the Spirit.*
—Galatians 5:24–25

Gain Understanding

Lay Aside—Self-indulgence
Put On—Obedience

Examine

1. Am I listening for God's voice so I know what He desires of me?
   How can I hear His voice? (See Psalm 19:1–2; John 10:27; John
   14:26; 2 Timothy 3:16–17, et al.)
2. What temptations am I failing to resist? Am I taking my thoughts
   captive to the obedience of Christ?
3. How can I walk as a slave of righteousness rather than a slave of
   sin?

Be Transformed

1 Samuel 15:22–23
Romans 6:16–18
2 Corinthians 10:5
Galatians 5:24–25
Hebrews 5:8–9
1 Peter 1:14–15

Pray

Jesus, You are the ultimate example of obedience—You were obedient
to the point of death! Again and again I fail to listen to and obey Your
voice and I present myself as a slave to sin. I would much rather be
a slave to You, for I know Your yoke is easy and Your load is light.
Thank You for setting me free from my sin by Your blood. Please
show me the way out of every temptation. Help me to resist fleshly
passions and desires and to walk by the Spirit.

31

ORDERLINESS
vs.
Disorganization

Preparing myself and
my surroundings so I will achieve
the greatest efficiency

But all things must be done properly and in an orderly manner.
—1 Corinthians 14:40

Gain Understanding

Lay Aside—Disorganization
Put On—Orderliness

Examine

1. Where can I recognize and be inspired by God's order in creation?
2. How does being disorganized hurt my family? How does it hurt me?
3. What do I miss out on when I am disorganized?

Be Transformed

Job 38
1 Corinthians 14:33
1 Corinthians 14:40

Pray

You are a God of peace and order, not confusion. When You created the world and all that is in it, You gave boundaries to the seas, You told the sun and stars when and where to shine, and You have a place to store snow, lightning, and rain. I struggle to keep my things where they belong and it disrupts the sense of peace and order in my home. I know that peace is the fruit of Your Spirit and disorganization makes it hard for me to feel or display Your peace. Please help me to keep everything in its place.

32

PATIENCE
vs.
Restlessness

Enduring troubles, especially those
caused by other people,
without complaining or retaliating

And not only this, but we also exult in our tribulations,
knowing that tribulation brings about perseverance; and
perseverance, proven character; and proven character, hope.
—Romans 5:3–4

Gain Understanding

Lay Aside—Restlessness
Put On—Patience

Examine

1. How can I use waiting on others as an opportunity to learn to wait on God?
2. What is the result of patiently enduring suffering?
3. When does God ask me to be patient?
4. How long am I expected to be patient?

Be Transformed

Psalm 40:1
Romans 5:3–4
Romans 12:12
James 5:7–8
1 Peter 2:23

Pray

God, You are so incredibly patient with us! I can be slow to learn, often making the same mistakes again and again and again, yet You do not grow restless with me. Jesus, when I face troubles caused by others, rather than becoming frustrated and lashing out, help me to follow Your example by entrusting myself to our Father. Help me to persevere in the challenges I face as I patiently wait for Your coming.

33

PEACEMAKING
vs.
Aggravating

Seeking, pursuing, and promoting
harmony in my relationships

Deceit is in the heart of those who devise evil,
but counselors of peace have joy.
—Proverbs 12:20

Gain Understanding

Lay Aside—Aggravating
Put On—Peacemaking

Examine

1. What is the result for me and others when I promote peace?
2. What kind of person am I being if I stir up strife? If I promote peace?
3. With whom does God expect me to do my best to live at peace?
4. How can I promote and pursue peace in my relationships?

Be Transformed

Proverbs 12:20
Proverbs 18:6
Matthew 5:9
Romans 12:18
1 Peter 3:11

Pray

Jesus, Prince of Peace, forgive me for aggravating! Forgive me for thinking I can find joy in aggravating when Your Word says peacemakers are the ones who have joy. I do not want to be foolish and stir up strife; I want to be a blessed child of God. Please show me how I can pursue and promote peace. I want to be a peacemaker.

34

PERSUASIVENESS
vs.
Contentiousness

Gently guiding vital truths
around another's mental roadblocks
without being insensitive or pushy

*The Lord's bond-servant must not be quarrelsome, but be kind
to all, able to teach, patient when wronged, with gentleness
correcting those who are in opposition, if perhaps God may grant
them repentance leading to the knowledge of the truth.*
—2 Timothy 2:24–25

Gain Understanding

Lay Aside—Contentiousness
Put On—Persuasiveness

Examine

1. How can I be bold about what I know to be true without being argumentative?
2. Who is it that begins and finishes good work in people?
3. Can I "prove" Truth? If not, what is my responsibility in persuading others of what is true?

Be Transformed

Acts 19:8–10
Philippians 1:6
2 Corinthians 3:5–6
2 Timothy 2:24–25

Pray

Jesus, You are so kind, patient, and gentle with people who do not fully understand what is true; You are never argumentative. I often fight so hard to get my point across without relying on You. You are the one who has the power to open blind eyes, not I. Help me to gently correct those who believe what is false and make me adequate as a servant of the gospel.

35

RESOURCEFULNESS
vs.
Wastefulness

Wise use of that
which others would normally
overlook or discard

*He who is faithful in a very little thing is faithful also in much; and he
who is unrighteous in a very little thing is unrighteous also in much.*
—Luke 16:10

Gain Understanding

Lay Aside—Wastefulness
Put On—Resourcefulness

Examine

1. Am I being careless with gifts God has given me because they are easily replaced?
2. Do I try to fix broken things and reuse or recycle when possible?
3. Do I see value and potential in objects, ideas, and people?
4. How can I make wise use of my time, talents, and energy?

Be Transformed

Matthew 25:14–30
John 6:12–13
Luke 16:10

Pray

Lord Jesus, You never overlook or discard that which is useful. You have given me many good and perfect gifts. Thank You! I confess at times I fail to see the potential in them and other times I just don't even care. May I never be wasteful. You spent much of Your time and energy investing in people. Help me follow Your example. I want to use and invest wisely all that You have given me.

36

RESPONSIBILITY
vs.
Unreliability

Recognizing and doing
what God and those in authority
over me require

*Therefore, to one who knows the right thing to
do and does not do it, to him it is sin.*
—James 4:17

Gain Understanding

Lay Aside—Unreliability
Put On—Responsibility

Examine

1. Do I know what would have been right in a particular situation when I was unreliable?
2. Whom do I burden when I do not do the things I should?
3. Who is responsible for my actions before God?

Be Transformed

Romans 14:12
Galatians 6:5
James 4:17

Pray

You are faithful, God, and I can always count on You to do what is good and right and to follow through with Your promises. I confess I burden others with my lack of responsibility and fail to do the things I know are right and good. Please help me to bear my own load and be responsible.

37

REVERENCE
vs.
Disrespect

Recognizing and honoring the
authority of God with awe and fear

*Therefore, since we receive a kingdom which cannot be shaken,
let us show gratitude, by which we may offer to God an acceptable
service with reverence and awe; for our God is a consuming fire.*
—Hebrews 12:28–29

Gain Understanding

Lay Aside—Disrespect
Put On—Reverence

Examine

1. How can the fear of the Lord protect me? How can disrespect put me in danger?
2. What happens to my heart when I choose disrespect over reverence?
3. What is different between the fear a believer feels versus the fear a nonbeliever feels toward God?
4. How does God deserve to be treated by me? How do I treat Him?
5. Is the fear of man leading me to dishonor God?

Be Transformed

1 Samuel 12:24
Proverbs 14:27
Matthew 10:28
Romans 1:21–23
Hebrews 12:28–29
1 John 4:18

Pray

You alone are God and worthy of honor, glory, and praise. My soul is in Your hands! Please forgive me for taking this truth so lightly and failing to show You the reverence You deserve. Thank You for promising me a kingdom that cannot be shaken. Protect me from the fear of man, and teach me to fear You in such a way that I serve and worship You with reverence and awe with all my heart.

38

SELF-CONTROL
vs.
Anger

Restraining my emotions and
actions when I feel provoked

A fool always loses his temper, but a wise man holds it back.
—Proverbs 29:11

Gain Understanding

Lay Aside—Anger
Put On—Self-control

Examine

1. What kind of person am I being if I am constantly losing my temper? If I restrain my anger?
2. God created me with two ears and one mouth. Which should be used more?
3. What have been the results when I have had outbursts of anger? How might things have turned out differently had I exercised self-control?

Be Transformed

Proverbs 12:16
Proverbs 14:29
Proverbs 29:11
Ecclesiastes 7:9
James 1:19–20

Pray

God, You are gracious and slow to anger. So often I display foolishness in easily losing my temper. Thank you for dying on the cross so that I have forgiveness for all my angry outbursts. I want to be wise and learn to hold my anger back. Please grow the fruit of self-control in my life.

39

SUBMISSION
vs.
Willfulness

Quickly and cheerfully
Carrying out the direction
of those who are responsible for me

Remind them to be subject to rulers, to authorities, to
be obedient, to be ready for every good deed.
—Titus 3:1

Gain Understanding

Lay Aside—Willfulness
Put On—Submission

Examine

1. Am I truly obeying when I obey with an unhappy heart?
2. Does God say it is hateful or loving for my parents to discipline me?
3. What is the result of disobedience? What is the result of submitting to discipline?

Be Transformed

Proverbs 13:13, 18, 24
Proverbs 15:32
Ephesians 6:1–3
Titus 3:1

Pray

Forgive me, Lord, for refusing to yield to those you have placed in authority over me. Thank You for giving me parents who love me enough to discipline me diligently. Help me to honor my parents and others You have put in charge of me by obeying all the way, right away, with a happy heart. I want to be ready for every good work You have for me!

40

THANKFULNESS
vs.
Complaining

Expressing appreciation
to God and others for ways
in which they have benefited my life

In everything give thanks; for this is God's will for you in Christ Jesus.
—1 Thessalonians 5:18

Gain Understanding

Lay Aside—Complaining
Put On—Thankfulness

Examine

1. When hard or bad things happen in my life, will grumbling or complaining help in any way?
2. When does God ask me to show thankfulness?
3. What can I express thankfulness for when nothing seems to be going right?
4. Who should I thank for every good thing in my life?

Be Transformed

1 Corinthians 10:10
Philippians 2:14
1 Thessalonians 5:18
Hebrews 13:15
James 1:17

Pray

I confess I have a habit of complaining! Jesus, when You were on this earth, You had so little and suffered so much, yet You never once grumbled. I have many good things in my life, and every one of them is a gift from You. Through You, I know I can give thanks in every circumstance.

41

THRIFTINESS
vs.
Extravagance

Not letting myself
or asking others to spend
that which is not necessary

Therefore if you have not been faithful in the use of unrighteous
wealth, who will entrust the true riches to you?
—Luke 16:11

Gain Understanding

Lay Aside—Extravagance
Put On—Thriftiness

Examine

1. Am I honoring God with the way I spend my resources (money, time, energy, etc.)? Am I giving Him the first and best or the leftovers?
2. What does extravagant spending on meaningless things lead to?
3. How can thriftiness benefit the kingdom of God?
4. Is extravagance always a negative thing?

Be Transformed

Genesis 41:34–36
Proverbs 3:9
Proverbs 28:19
Matthew 26:6–10
Luke 16:11

Pray

Lord, the entire world and all that is in it belongs to You. Forgive me for wasting the resources You have entrusted to me on things that are fading away, on my own selfish desires. Thank you for the extravagant ways You provide for me. Help me to honor You with the best of all You have given me. Allow Your extravagant love to flow through me to others.

42

TOLERANCE
vs.
Prejudice

Acceptance of others
as unique creations of God
in varying degrees of maturity

Therefore, accept one another, just as Christ
also accepted us to the glory of God.
—Romans 15:7

Gain Understanding

Lay Aside—Prejudice
Put On—Tolerance

Examine

1. Is my attitude toward others in line with Jesus's?
2. Am I forming an opinion about someone without having sufficient knowledge?
3. Am I called to tolerate sin? To condemn those who sin? What am I called to do when it comes to judging others and their actions?

Be Transformed

Matthew 9:10–12
John 8:7–11
Romans 15:7
Galatians 6:1

Pray

Jesus, You so freely accepted men, women, and children in all states and stages of life. I confess I sometimes form judgments against people without having just grounds and sufficient knowledge. Thank You for accepting me and dying for me while I was yet a sinner. Help me to accept others to the glory of God. Teach me how not to condemn others who are in the midst of sin, how to bear gently with them, and yet not show tolerance toward their sin.

43

TRUST
vs.
Anxiety

Confident rest
In God's character, His promises,
and His love for me

Be anxious for nothing, but in everything by prayer and
supplication with thanksgiving let your requests be made known
to God. And the peace of God, which surpasses all comprehension,
will guard your hearts and your minds in Christ Jesus.
—Philippians 4:6–7

Gain Understanding

Lay Aside—Anxiety
Put On—Trust

Examine

1. What is the result of really trusting in God?
2. What is the most valuable part of God's creation? How does He care for the less valuable parts of creation? How will He care for me?
3. What should I do when I feel anxious?
4. How can thankfulness defeat anxiety?
5. Does anything good come from worrying?

Be Transformed

Isaiah 26:3
Matthew 6:25–27
Philippians 4:6–7
1 Peter 5:7

Pray

Father, You are completely trustworthy. Why do I focus on my trials and troubles rather than on You, my Creator who loves and cares for me? Thank You for Your faithfulness to provide for my every need. Please cause anxiety to trigger me to pray to You. Remind me of all the things I have to be thankful for and guard my heart and mind in Christ Jesus.

44

VIRTUE
vs.
Impurity

The moral excellence and purity
of spirit that radiate from my life
as I obey God's Word

*Seeing that His divine power has granted to us everything
pertaining to life and godliness, through the true knowledge
of Him who called us by His own glory and excellence.*
—2 Peter 1:3

Gain Understanding

Lay Aside—Impurity
Put On—Virtue

Examine

1. Am I fleeing impurity or allowing myself to flirt with impurity, whether in thought or deed?
2. What kind of things am I thinking about and dwelling on? How is this affecting my actions?
3. Am I guarding my eyes, ears, thoughts, and words?
4. When I feel overwhelmed by temptation and virtue seems impossible, what truth can I cling to?

Be Transformed

Isaiah 33:14–16
1 Corinthians 3:16–17
Philippians 4:8
2 Timothy 2:22
2 Peter 1:3

Pray

God, You are holy, holy, holy. There is no darkness in You. Forgive me for the impurity and wickedness of my thoughts, words, and actions. Thank You, Jesus, that because of the blood You shed for me, I am made holy. Help me to work out this truth that You have worked in me. Strengthen me to be able to flee lust and to pursue righteousness, faith, love, and peace. May my body, the temple of Your Spirit, be a place You are pleased to dwell.

45

WISDOM
vs.
Foolishness

Seeing and responding
to life's situations from
God's frame of reference

Trust in the LORD with all your heart and do not lean on
your own understanding. In all your ways acknowledge Him,
and He will make your paths straight. Do not be wise in
your own eyes; fear the LORD and turn away from evil.
—Proverbs 3:5–7

Gain Understanding

Lay Aside—Foolishness
Put On—Wisdom

Examine

1. Where can I gain wisdom?
2. Does foolishness ever bring about positive results?
3. Why is it important to choose my friends carefully?
4. Am I quick to accept counsel, or even correction, from a wise person?

Be Transformed

Proverbs 3:5–7
Proverbs 9:10
Proverbs 13:20
Proverbs 17:12
Psalm 119:98
1 Corinthians 3:19

Pray

You, God, are the source of all true wisdom. So frequently I behave foolishly and lean on my own understanding instead of seeking Your wisdom. Thank You for Your promise to give me wisdom from above when I ask. Help me to choose wise friends. Remind me to acknowledge You in all my ways, and I will trust You to make my path straight.

QUICK-REFERENCE
SCRIPTURE GUIDE

Aggravating vs. Peacemaking

Proverbs 12:20 "Deceit is in the heart of those who devise evil, but counselors of peace have joy."

Proverbs 18:6 "A fool's lips bring strife, and his mouth calls for blows."

Matthew 5:9 "Blessed are the peacemakers, for they shall be called sons of God."

Romans 12:18 "If possible, so far as it depends on you, be at peace with all men."

1 Peter 3:11 "He must turn away from evil and do good; he must seek peace and pursue it."

Aloofness vs. Hospitality

Matthew 25:35–40 "'For I was hungry, and you gave Me something to eat; I was thirsty, and you gave Me something to drink; I was a stranger, and you invited Me in; naked, and you clothed Me; I was sick, and you visited Me; I was in prison, and you came to Me.' Then the righteous will answer Him, 'Lord, when did we see You hungry, and feed You, or thirsty, and give You something to drink? And when did we see You a stranger, and invite You in, or naked, and clothe You? When did we see You sick, or in prison, and come to You?' The King will answer and say to them, 'Truly I say to you, to the extent that you did it to one of these brothers of Mine, even the least of them, you did it to Me.'"

Romans 12:13 ". . . contributing to the needs of the saints, practicing hospitality."

Hebrews 13:2 "Do not neglect to show hospitality to strangers, for by this some have entertained angels without knowing it."

1 Peter 4:9 "Be hospitable to one another without complaint."

Anger vs. Self-control

Proverbs 12:16 "A fool's anger is known at once, but a prudent man conceals dishonor."

Proverbs 14:29 "He who is slow to anger has great understanding, but he who is quick-tempered exalts folly."

Proverbs 29:11 "A fool always loses his temper, but a wise man holds it back."

Ecclesiastes 7:9 "Do not be eager in your heart to be angry, for anger resides in the bosom of fools."

James 1:19–20 "This you know, my beloved brethren. But everyone must be quick to hear, slow to speak and slow to anger; for the anger of man does not achieve the righteousness of God."

Anxiety vs. Trust

Isaiah 26:3 "The steadfast of mind You will keep in perfect peace, because he trusts in You."

Matthew 6:25–27 "For this reason I say to you, do not be worried about your life, as to what you will eat or what you will drink; nor for your body, as to what you will put on. Is not life more than food, and the body more than clothing? Look at the birds of the air, that they do not sow, nor reap nor gather into barns, and yet your heavenly Father feeds them. Are you not worth much more than they? And who of you by being worried can add a single hour to his life?"

Philippians 4:6-7 "Be anxious for nothing, but in everything by prayer and supplication with thanksgiving let your requests be made known to God. And the peace of God, which surpasses all comprehension, will guard your hearts and your minds in Christ Jesus."

1 Peter 5:7 ". . . casting all your anxiety on Him, because He cares for you."

Apathy vs. Enthusiasm

Romans 12:11 ". . . not lagging behind in diligence, fervent in spirit, serving the Lord."

2 Corinthians 6:10 ". . . as sorrowful yet always rejoicing, as poor yet making many rich, as having nothing yet possessing all things."

Philippians 4:4 "Rejoice in the Lord always; again I will say, rejoice!"

1 Thessalonians 5:16 "Rejoice always;"

Titus 2:13–14 ". . . looking for the blessed hope and the appearing of the glory of our great God and Savior, Christ Jesus, who gave Himself for us to redeem us from every lawless deed, and to purify for Himself a people for His own possession, zealous for good deeds."

Bitterness vs. Forgiveness

Matthew 18:15–16 "If your brother sins, go and show him his fault in private; if he listens to you, you have won your brother. But if he does not listen to you, take one or two more with you, so that by the mouth of two or three witnesses every fact may be confirmed."

Matthew 18:21–22 "Then Peter came and said to Him, 'Lord, how often shall my brother sin against me and I forgive him? Up to seven times?' Jesus said to him, 'I do not say to you, up to seven times, but up to seventy times seven.'"

Romans 12:21 "Do not be overcome by evil, but overcome evil with good."

Ephesians 4:32 "Be kind to one another, tender-hearted, forgiving each other, just as God in Christ also has forgiven you."

Colossians 3:13 ". . . bearing with one another, and forgiving each other, whoever has a complaint against anyone; just as the Lord forgave you, so also should you."

1 Peter 3:9 ". . . not returning evil for evil or insult for insult, but giving a blessing instead; for you were called for the very purpose that you might inherit a blessing."

Carelessness vs. Discretion

Proverbs 11:13 "He who goes about as a talebearer reveals secrets, but he who is trustworthy conceals a matter."

Proverbs 13:3 "The one who guards his mouth preserves his life; the one who opens wide his lips comes to ruin."

Proverbs 14:16 "A wise man is cautious and turns away from evil, but a fool is arrogant and careless."

Proverbs 20:19 "He who goes about as a slanderer reveals secrets, therefore do not associate with a gossip."

Proverbs 22:3 "The prudent sees the evil and hides himself, But the naive go on, and are punished for it."

Matthew 12:36–37 "But I tell you that every careless word that people speak, they shall give an accounting for it in the day of judgment. For by your words you will be justified, and by your words you will be condemned."

Complaining vs. Thankfulness

1 Corinthians 10:10 "Nor grumble, as some of them did, and were destroyed by the destroyer."

Philippians 2:14 "Do all things without grumbling or disputing."

1 Thessalonians 5:18 ". . . in everything give thanks; for this is God's will for you in Christ Jesus."

Hebrews 13:15 "Through Him then, let us continually offer up a sacrifice of praise to God, that is, the fruit of lips that give thanks to His name."

James 1:17 "Every good thing given and every perfect gift is from above, coming down from the Father of lights, with whom there is no variation or shifting shadow."

Contentiousness vs. Persuasiveness

Acts 19:8–10 "And he entered the synagogue and continued speaking out boldly for three months, reasoning and persuading them about the kingdom of God. But when some were becoming hardened and disobedient, speaking evil of the Way before the people, he withdrew from them and took away the disciples, reasoning daily in the school of Tyrannus. This took place for two years, so that all who lived in Asia heard the word of the Lord, both Jews and Greeks."

Philippians 1:6 "For I am confident of this very thing, that He who began a good work in you will perfect it until the day of Christ Jesus."

2 Corinthians 3:5–6 "Not that we are adequate in ourselves to consider anything as coming from ourselves, but our adequacy is from God, who also made us adequate as servants of a new covenant, not of the letter but of the Spirit; for the letter kills, but the Spirit gives life."

2 Timothy 2:24–25 "The Lord's bond-servant must not be quarrelsome, but be kind to all, able to teach, patient when wronged, with gentleness correcting those who are in opposition, if perhaps God may grant them repentance leading to the knowledge of the truth."

Covetousness vs. Contentment

Exodus 20:17 "You shall not covet your neighbor's house; you shall not covet your neighbor's wife or his male servant or his female servant or his ox or his donkey or anything that belongs to your neighbor."

Luke 12:15 "Then He said to them, 'Beware, and be on your guard against every form of greed; for not even when one has an abundance does his life consist of his possessions.'"

Philippians 4:11–12 "Not that I speak from want, for I have learned to be content in whatever circumstances I am. I know how to get along with humble means, and I also know how to live in prosperity; in any and every circumstance I have learned the secret of being filled and going hungry, both of having abundance and suffering need."

1 Timothy 6:8 "If we have food and covering, with these we shall be content."

Hebrews 13:5 "Make sure that your character is free from the love of money, being content with what you have; for He Himself has said, 'I will never desert you, nor will I ever forsake you.'"

1 John 2:15 "Do not love the world nor the things in the world. If anyone loves the world, the love of the Father is not in him."

Cruelty vs. Kindness

Proverbs 3:3 "Do not let kindness and truth leave you; bind them around your neck, write them on the tablet of your heart."

Proverbs 11:17 "The merciful man does himself good, but the cruel man does himself harm."

Matthew 7:12 "In everything, therefore, treat people the same way you want them to treat you, for this is the Law and the Prophets."

Luke 6:35 "But love your enemies, and do good, and lend, expecting nothing in return; and your reward will be great, and you will be sons of the Most High; for He Himself is kind to ungrateful and evil men."

Deception vs. Honesty

Proverbs 6:16–17 "There are six things which the Lord hates, yes, seven which are an abomination to Him: haughty eyes, a lying tongue, and hands that shed innocent blood."

Proverbs 12:22 "Lying lips are an abomination to the Lord, but those who deal faithfully are His delight."

Mark 7:21–22 "For from within, out of the heart of men, proceed the evil thoughts, fornications, thefts, murders, adulteries, deeds of coveting and wickedness, as well as deceit, sensuality, envy, slander, pride and foolishness."

John 8:44 "You are of your father, the devil, and you want to do the desires of your father. He was a murderer from the beginning, and has not stood in the truth because there is no truth in him. Whenever he speaks a lie, he speaks from his own nature, for he is a liar and the father of lies."

Ephesians 4:25 "Therefore, laying aside falsehood, SPEAK TRUTH EACH ONE of you WITH HIS NEIGHBOR, for we are members of one another."

Discouragement vs. Determination

Matthew 26:38–39 "Then He said to them, 'My soul is deeply grieved, to the point of death; remain here and keep watch with Me.' And He went a little beyond them, and fell on His face and prayed, saying, 'My Father, if it is possible, let this cup pass from Me; yet not as I will, but as You will.'"

Galatians 6:9 "Let us not lose heart in doing good, for in due time we will reap if we do not grow weary."

Philippians 4:13 "I can do all things through Him who strengthens me."

2 Thessalonians 3:13 "But as for you brethren, do not grow weary of doing good."

Hebrews 12:3 "For consider Him who has endured such hostility by sinners against Himself, so that you will not grow weary and lose heart."

Disorganization vs. Orderliness

Job 38 "Then the Lord answered Job out of the whirlwind and said,
'Who is this that darkens counsel
by words without knowledge?
Now gird up your loins like a man,
and I will ask you, and you instruct Me!
Where were you when I laid the foundation of the earth?
Tell Me, if you have understanding,
who set its measurements? Since you know.
Or who stretched the line on it?
On what were its bases sunk?
Or who laid its cornerstone,
when the morning stars sang together
and all the sons of God shouted for joy?

Or who enclosed the sea with doors
when, bursting forth, it went out from the womb;
when I made a cloud its garment
and thick darkness its swaddling band,
and I placed boundaries on it
and set a bolt and doors,
and I said, "Thus far you shall come, but no farther;
and here shall your proud waves stop."
Have you ever in your life commanded the morning,
and caused the dawn to know its place,
that it might take hold of the ends of the earth,
and the wicked be shaken out of it?
It is changed like clay under the seal;
and they stand forth like a garment.
From the wicked their light is withheld,
and the uplifted arm is broken.

Have you entered into the springs of the sea
or walked in the recesses of the deep?
Have the gates of death been revealed to you,
or have you seen the gates of deep darkness?
Have you understood the expanse of the earth?
Tell Me, if you know all this.

Where is the way to the dwelling of light?
and darkness, where is its place,
that you may take it to its territory
and that you may discern the paths to its home?
You know, for you were born then,
and the number of your days is great!
Have you entered the storehouses of the snow,
or have you seen the storehouses of the hail,
which I have reserved for the time of distress,
for the day of war and battle?
Where is the way that the light is divided,
or the east wind scattered on the earth?

Who has cleft a channel for the flood,
or a way for the thunderbolt,
to bring rain on a land without people,
on a desert without a man in it,
to satisfy the waste and desolate land
and to make the seeds of grass to sprout?
Has the rain a father?
Or who has begotten the drops of dew?
From whose womb has come the ice?
And the frost of heaven, who has given it birth?
Water becomes hard like stone,
and the surface of the deep is imprisoned.

Can you bind the chains of the Pleiades,
or loose the cords of Orion?
Can you lead forth a constellation in its season,
and guide the Bear with her satellites?
Do you know the ordinances of the heavens,
or fix their rule over the earth?

Can you lift up your voice to the clouds,
so that an abundance of water will cover you?
Can you send forth lightnings that they may go
and say to you, "Here we are"?
Who has put wisdom in the innermost being
or given understanding to the mind?
Who can count the clouds by wisdom,
or tip the water jars of the heavens,
When the dust hardens into a mass
and the clods stick together?
Can you hunt the prey for the lion, or satisfy
the appetite of the young lions,
When they crouch in their dens and lie in wait in their lair?
Who prepares for the raven its nourishment
when its young cry to God and wander about without food?'"

1 Corinthians 14:33 ". . . for God is not a God of confusion but of peace, as in all the churches of the saints."
1 Corinthians 14:40 "But all things must be done properly and in an orderly manner."

Disrespect vs. Reverence

1 Samuel 12:24 "Only fear the Lord and serve Him in truth with all your heart; for consider what great things He has done for you."
Proverbs 14:27 "The fear of the Lord is a fountain of life, that one may avoid the snares of death."

Matthew 10:28 "Do not fear those who kill the body but are unable to kill the soul; but rather fear Him who is able to destroy both soul and body in hell."

Romans 1:21–23 "For even though they knew God, they did not honor Him as God or give thanks, but they became futile in their speculations, and their foolish heart was darkened. Professing to be wise, they became fools, and exchanged the glory of the incorruptible God for an image in the form of corruptible man and of birds and four-footed animals and crawling creatures."

Hebrews 12:28–29 "Therefore, since we receive a kingdom which cannot be shaken, let us show gratitude, by which we may offer to God an acceptable service with reverence and awe; for our God is a consuming fire."

1 John 4:18 "There is no fear in love; but perfect love casts out fear, because fear involves punishment, and the one who fears is not perfected in love."

Double-mindedness vs. Decisiveness

Proverbs 19:20 "Listen to counsel and accept discipline, that you may be wise the rest of your days."

Romans 12:2 "And do not be conformed to this world, but be transformed by the renewing of your mind, so that you may prove what the will of God is, that which is good and acceptable and perfect."

2 Corinthians 10:5 "We are destroying speculations and every lofty thing raised up against the knowledge of God, and we are taking every thought captive to the obedience of Christ."

James 1:5 "But if any of you lacks wisdom, let him ask of God, who gives to all generously and without reproach, and it will be given to him."

James 1:6–8 "But he must ask in faith without any doubting, for the one who doubts is like the surf of the sea, driven and tossed by the wind. For that man ought not to expect that he will receive anything from the Lord, being a double-minded man, unstable in all his ways."

Extravagance vs. Thriftiness

Genesis 41:34–36 "Let Pharaoh take action to appoint overseers in charge of the land, and let him exact a fifth of the produce of the land of Egypt in the seven years of abundance. Then let them gather all the food of these good years that are coming, and store up the grain for food in the cities under Pharaoh's authority, and let them guard it. Let the food become as a reserve for the land for the seven years of famine which will occur in the land of Egypt, so that the land will not perish during the famine."

Proverbs 3:9 "Honor the Lord from your wealth and from the first of all your produce."

Proverbs 28:19 "He who tills his land will have plenty of food, but he who follows empty pursuits will have poverty in plenty."

Matthew 26:6–10 "Now when Jesus was in Bethany, at the home of Simon the leper, a woman came to Him with an alabaster vial of very costly perfume, and she poured it on His head as He reclined at the table. But the disciples were indignant when they saw this, and said, 'Why this waste? For this perfume might have been sold for a high price and the money given to the poor.' But Jesus, aware of this, said to them, 'Why do you bother the woman? For she has done a good deed to Me.'"

Luke 16:11 "Therefore if you have not been faithful in the use of unrighteous wealth, who will entrust the true riches to you?"

Fearfulness vs. Boldness

Deuteronomy 31:6 "Be strong and courageous, do not be afraid or tremble at them, for the Lord your God is the one who goes with you. He will not fail you or forsake you."

Proverbs 29:25 "The fear of man brings a snare, but he who trusts in the Lord will be exalted."

Matthew 8:26 "He said to them, 'Why are you afraid, you men of little faith?' Then He got up and rebuked the winds and the sea, and it became perfectly calm."

Acts 4:29 "And now, Lord, take note of their threats, and grant that Your bond-servants may speak Your word with all confidence."

2 Timothy 1:7 For "God has not given us a spirit of timidity, but of power and love and discipline."

Foolishness vs. Wisdom

Proverbs 3:5–7 "Trust in the LORD with all your heart and do not lean on your own understanding. In all your ways acknowledge Him, and He will make your paths straight. Do not be wise in your own eyes; fear the LORD and turn away from evil."

Proverbs 9:10 "The fear of the LORD is the beginning of wisdom, and the knowledge of the Holy One is understanding."

Proverbs 13:20 "He who walks with wise men will be wise, but the companion of fools will suffer harm."

Proverbs 17:12 "Let a man meet a bear robbed of her cubs, rather than a fool in his folly."

Psalm 119:98 "Your commandments make me wiser than my enemies, for they are ever mine."

1 Corinthians 3:19 "For the wisdom of this world is foolishness before God. For it is written, 'He is THE ONE WHO CATCHES THE WISE IN THEIR CRAFTINESS'"

Harshness vs. Gentleness

Proverbs 15:1 "A gentle answer turns away wrath, but a harsh word stirs up anger."

Matthew 5:5 "Blessed are the gentle, for they shall inherit the earth."

Philippians 4:5 "Let your gentle spirit be known to all men. The Lord is near."

1 Thessalonians 2:7 "But we proved to be gentle among you, as a nursing mother tenderly cares for her own children."

Haste vs. Cautiousness

Proverbs 19:2 "Also it is not good for a person to be without knowledge, and he who hurries his footsteps errs."

Proverbs 21:5 "The plans of the diligent lead surely to advantage, but everyone who is hasty comes surely to poverty."

Proverbs 29:20 "Do you see a man who is hasty in his words? There is more hope for a fool than for him."

Luke 14:28 "For which one of you, when he wants to build a tower, does not first sit down and calculate the cost to see if he has enough to complete it?"

James 1:19 "This you know, my beloved brethren. But everyone must be quick to hear, slow to speak and slow to anger."

Hypocrisy vs. Integrity

Proverbs 11:3 "The integrity of the upright will guide them, but the crookedness of the treacherous will destroy them."

Matthew 23:27–28 "Woe to you, scribes and Pharisees, hypocrites! For you are like whitewashed tombs which on the outside appear beautiful, but inside they are full of dead men's bones and all uncleanness. So you, too, outwardly appear righteous to men, but inwardly you are full of hypocrisy and lawlessness."

2 Corinthians 1:12 "For our proud confidence is this: the testimony of our conscience, that in holiness and godly sincerity, not in fleshly wisdom but in the grace of God, we have conducted ourselves in the world, and especially toward you."

Galatians 2:13 "The rest of the Jews joined him in hypocrisy, with the result that even Barnabas was carried away by their hypocrisy."

1 John 1:9 "If we confess our sins, He is faithful and righteous to forgive us our sins and to cleanse us from all unrighteousness."

Impurity vs. Virtue

Isaih 33:14–16 "Sinners in Zion are terrified; trembling has seized the godless. 'Who among us can live with the consuming fire? Who among us can live with continual burning?' He who walks righteously and speaks with sincerity, He who rejects unjust gain and shakes his hands so that they hold no bribe; He who stops his ears from hearing about bloodshed and shuts his eyes from looking upon evil; He will dwell on the heights, His refuge will be the impregnable rock; His bread will be given him, His water will be sure."

1 Corinthians 3:16–17 "Do you not know that you are a temple of God and that the Spirit of God dwells in you? If any man destroys the temple of God, God will destroy him, for the temple of God is holy, and that is what you are."

Philippians 4:8 "Finally, brethren, whatever is true, whatever is honorable, whatever is right, whatever is pure, whatever is lovely, whatever is of good repute, if there is any excellence and if anything worthy of praise, dwell on these things."

2 Timothy 2:22 "Now flee from youthful lusts and pursue righteousness, faith, love and peace, with those who call on the Lord from a pure heart."

2 Peter 1:3 ". . . seeing that His divine power has granted to us everything pertaining to life and godliness, through the true knowledge of Him who called us by His own glory and excellence."

Inconsistency vs. Faithfulness

Numbers 30:2 "If a man makes a vow to the LORD, or takes an oath to bind himself with a binding obligation, he shall not violate his word; he shall do according to all that proceeds out of his mouth."

Psalm 15:4 "In whose eyes a reprobate is despised, but who honors those who fear the Lord; He swears to his own hurt and does not change."

Matthew 25:23 "His master said to him, 'Well done, good and faithful slave. You were faithful with a few things, I will put you in charge of many things; enter into the joy of your master.'"

Revelation 2:10 "Do not fear what you are about to suffer. Behold, the devil is about to cast some of you into prison, so that you will be tested, and you will have tribulation for ten days. Be faithful until death, and I will give you the crown of life."

Indifference vs. Compassion

Job 6:14 "For the despairing man there should be kindness from his friend; So that he does not forsake the fear of the Almighty."

2 Corinthians 1:3–4 "Blessed be the God and Father of our Lord Jesus Christ, the Father of mercies and God of all comfort, who comforts us in all our affliction so that we will be able to comfort those who are in any affliction with the comfort with which we ourselves are comforted by God."

Galatians 6:2 "Bear one another's burdens, and thereby fulfill the law of Christ."

1 John 3:17 "But whoever has the world's goods, and sees his brother in need and closes his heart against him, how does the love of God abide in him?"

Judgment vs. Discernment

1 Samuel 16:7 "But the Lord said to Samuel, 'Do not look at his appearance or at the height of his stature, because I have rejected him; for God sees not as man sees, for man looks at the outward appearance, but the Lord looks at the heart.'"

Luke 6:41–42 "Why do you look at the speck that is in your brother's eye, but do not notice the log that is in your own eye? Or how can you say to your brother, 'Brother, let me take out the speck that is in your eye,' when you yourself do not see the log that is in your own eye? You hypocrite, first take the log out of your own eye, and then you will see clearly to take out the speck that is in your brother's eye."

Hebrews 5:13–14 "For everyone who partakes only of milk is not accustomed to the word of righteousness, for he is an infant. But solid food is for the mature, who because of practice have their senses trained to discern good and evil."

Laziness vs. Diligence

Proverbs 12:24 "The hand of the diligent will rule, but the slack hand will be put to forced labor."

Proverbs 13:4 "The soul of the sluggard craves and gets nothing, but the soul of the diligent is made fat."

Ephesians 2:10 "For we are His workmanship, created in Christ Jesus for good works, which God prepared beforehand so that we would walk in them."

Colossians 3:23–24 "Whatever you do, do your work heartily, as for the Lord rather than for men, knowing that from the Lord you will receive the reward of the inheritance. It is the Lord Christ whom you serve."

Hebrews 6:10–12 "For God is not unjust so as to forget your work and the love which you have shown toward His name, in having ministered and in still ministering to the saints. And we desire that each one of you show the same diligence so as to realize the full assurance of hope until the end, so that you will not be sluggish, but imitators of those who through faith and patience inherit the promises."

Prejudice vs. Tolerance

Matthew 9:10–12 "Then it happened that as Jesus was reclining at the table in the house, behold, many tax collectors and sinners came and were dining with Jesus and His disciples. When the Pharisees saw this, they said to His disciples, 'Why is your Teacher eating with the tax collectors and sinners?' But when Jesus heard this, He said, 'It is not those who are healthy who need a physician, but those who are sick.'"

John 8:7–11 "But when they persisted in asking Him, He straightened up, and said to them, 'He who is without sin among you, let him be the first to throw a stone at her.' Straightening up, Jesus said to her, 'Woman, where are they? Did no one condemn you?' She said, 'No one, Lord.' And Jesus said, 'I do not condemn you, either. Go. From now on sin no more.'"

Romans 15:7 "Therefore, accept one another, just as Christ also accepted us to the glory of God."

Galatians 6:1 "Brethren, even if anyone is caught in any trespass, you who are spiritual, restore such a one in a spirit of gentleness; each one looking to yourself, so that you too will not be tempted."

Pride vs. Humility

Proverbs 25:27 "It is not good to eat much honey, nor is it glory to search out one's own glory."

Proverbs 27:2 "Let another praise you, and not your own mouth; a stranger, and not your own lips."

Luke 14:11 "For everyone who exalts himself will be humbled, and he who humbles himself will be exalted."

2 Corinthians 10:18 "For it is not he who commends himself that is approved, but he whom the Lord commends."

James 4:6 "But He gives a greater grace. Therefore it says, 'GOD IS OPPOSED TO THE PROUD, BUT GIVES GRACE TO THE HUMBLE.'"

Resistance vs. Flexibility

Psalm 145:17 "The Lord is righteous in all His ways and kind in all His deeds."

Colossians 3:2 "Set your mind on the things above, not on the things that are on earth."

2 Timothy 2:3–4 "Suffer hardship with me, as a good soldier of Christ Jesus. No soldier in active service entangles himself in the affairs of everyday life, so that he may please the one who enlisted him as a soldier."

James 4:13–15 "Come now, you who say, 'Today or tomorrow we will go to such and such a city, and spend a year there and engage in business and make a profit.' Yet you do not know what your life will be like tomorrow. You are just a vapor that appears for a little while and then vanishes away. Instead, you ought to say, 'If the Lord wills, we will live and also do this or that.'"

Restlessness vs. Patience

Psalm 40:1 "Wait for the Lord; be strong and let your heart take courage; yes, wait for the Lord."

Romans 5:3–4 "And not only this, but we also exult in our tribulations, knowing that tribulation brings about perseverance; and perseverance, proven character; and proven character, hope."

Romans 12:12 ". . . rejoicing in hope, persevering in tribulation, devoted to prayer."

James 5:7–8 "Therefore be patient, brethren, until the coming of the Lord. The farmer waits for the precious produce of the soil, being patient about it, until it gets the early and late rains. You too be patient; strengthen your hearts, for the coming of the Lord I near."

1 Peter 2:23 ". . . and while being reviled, He did not revile in return; while suffering, He uttered no threats, but kept entrusting Himself to Him who judges righteously."

Rudeness vs. Deference

Romans 12:10 "Be devoted to one another in brotherly love; give preference to one another in honor."

Romans 14:21 "It is good not to eat meat or to drink wine, or to do anything by which your brother stumbles."

1 Corinthians 8:9 "But take care that this liberty of yours does not somehow become a stumbling block to the weak."

1 Corinthians 8:13 "Therefore, if food causes my brother to stumble, I will never eat meat again, so that I will not cause my brother to stumble."

Self-centeredness vs. Availability

Isaiah 6:8 "Then I heard the voice of the Lord, saying, 'Whom shall I send, and who will go for Us?' Then I said, 'Here am I. Send me!'"

Romans 12:1 "Therefore I urge you, brethren, by the mercies of God, to present your bodies a living and holy sacrifice, acceptable to God, which is your spiritual service of worship."

1 Corinthians 6:20 "For you have been bought with a price: therefore glorify God in your body."

2 Corinthians 5:15 ". . . and He died for all, so that they who live might no longer live for themselves, but for Him who died and rose again on their behalf."

Philippians 2:20–21 "For I have no one else of kindred spirit who will genuinely be concerned for your welfare. For they all seek after their own interests, not those of Christ Jesus."

Self-indulgence vs. Obedience

1 Samuel 15:22–23 "Samuel said, 'Has the LORD as much delight in burnt offerings and sacrifices as in obeying the voice of the LORD? Behold, to obey is better than sacrifice, And to heed

than the fat of rams. For rebellion is as the sin of divination, and insubordination is as iniquity and idolatry. Because you have rejected the word of the LORD, He has also rejected you from being king.'"

Romans 6:16–18 "Do you not know that when you present yourselves to someone as slaves for obedience, you are slaves of the one whom you obey, either of sin resulting in death, or of obedience resulting in righteousness? But thanks be to God that though you were slaves of sin, you became obedient from the heart to that form of teaching to which you were committed, and having been freed from sin, you became slaves of righteousness."

2 Corinthians 10:5 "We are destroying speculations and every lofty thing raised up against the knowledge of God, and we are taking every thought captive to the obedience of Christ."

Galatians 5:24–25 "Now those who belong to Christ Jesus have crucified the flesh with its passions and desires. If we live by the Spirit, let us also walk by the Spirit."

Hebrews 5:8–9 "Although He was a Son, He learned obedience from the things which He suffered. And having been made perfect, He became to all those who obey Him the source of eternal salvation,"

1 Peter 1:14–15 "As obedient children, do not be conformed to the former lusts which were yours in your ignorance, but like the Holy One who called you, be holy yourselves also in all your behavior."

Selfishness vs. Love

John 15:13 "Greater love has no one than this, that one lay down his life for his friends."

1 Corinthians 13:3 "And if I give all my possessions to feed the poor, and if I surrender my body to be burned, but do not have love, it profits me nothing."

1 Corinthians 13:4–7 "Love is patient, love is kind and is not jealous; love does not brag and is not arrogant, does not act unbecomingly;

it does not seek its own, is not provoked, does not take into
account a wrong suffered, does not rejoice in unrighteousness,
but rejoices with the truth; bears all things, believes all things,
hopes all things, endures all things."

1 John 3:16 "We know love by this, that He laid down His life for us;
and we ought to lay down our lives for the brethren."

1 John 4:19 "We love, because He first loved us."

Self-pity vs. Joy

Psalm 16:11 "You will make known to me the path of life; In Your
presence is fullness of joy; In Your right hand there are pleasures
forever."

Psalm 21:6 "For You make him most blessed forever; You make him
joyful with gladness in Your presence."

John 3:29 "He who has the bride is the bridegroom; but the friend
of the bridegroom, who stands and hears him, rejoices greatly
because of the bridegroom's voice. So this joy of mine has been
made full."

James 1:2 "Consider it all joy, my brethren, when you encounter
various trials,"

1 Peter 1:3–6 "Blessed be the God and Father of our Lord Jesus Christ,
who according to His great mercy has caused us to be born again
to a living hope through the resurrection of Jesus Christ from
the dead, to obtain an inheritance which is imperishable and
undefiled and will not fade away, reserved in heaven for you, who
are protected by the power of God through faith for a salvation
ready to be revealed in the last time. In this you greatly rejoice,
even though now for a little while, if necessary, you have been
distressed by various trials."

Stinginess vs. Generosity

Psalm 24:1 "The earth is the Lord's, and all it contains, the world, and those who dwell in it."

Proverbs 11:24–25 "There is one who scatters, and yet increases all the more, and there is one who withholds what is justly due, and yet it results only in want. The generous man will be prosperous, and he who waters will himself be watered."

Matthew 7:9–11 "Or what man is there among you who, when his son asks for a loaf, will give him a stone? Or if he asks for a fish, he will not give him a snake, will he? If you then, being evil, know how to give good gifts to your children, how much more will your Father who is in heaven give what is good to those who ask Him!"

2 Corinthians 9:6–7 "Now this I say, he who sows sparingly will also reap sparingly, and he who sows bountifully will also reap bountifully. Each one must do just as he has purposed in his heart, not grudgingly or under compulsion, for God loves a cheerful giver."

Tearing Down vs. Edifying

Proverbs 26:18–19 "Like a madman who throws Firebrands, arrows and death, so is the man who deceives his neighbor, and says, 'Was I not joking?'"

Ephesians 4:8,11–12 "And He gave some as apostles, and some as prophets, and some as evangelists, and some as pastors and teachers, for the equipping of the saints for the work of service, to the building up of the body of Christ."

Eph 4:29 "Let no unwholesome word proceed from your mouth, but only such a word as is good for edification according to the need of the moment, so that it will give grace to those who hear."

1 Thessalonians 5:11 "Therefore encourage one another and build up one another, just as you also are doing."

Unawareness vs. Alertness

Mark 14:38 "Keep watching and praying that you may not come into temptation; the spirit is willing, but the flesh is weak."

1 Corinthians 16:13 "Be on the alert, stand firm in the faith, act like men, be strong."

1 Thessalonians 5:6 ". . . so then let us not sleep as others do, but let us be alert and sober."

1 Peter 5:8 "Be of sober spirit, be on the alert. Your adversary, the devil, prowls around like a roaring lion, seeking someone to devour."

Unbelief vs. Faith

Mark 9:24 "Immediately the boy's father cried out and said, 'I do believe; help my unbelief.'"

Romans 12:3 "For through the grace given to me I say to everyone among you not to think more highly of himself than he ought to think; but to think so as to have sound judgment, as God has allotted to each a measure of faith."

2 Corinthians 4:18 ". . . while we look not at the things which are seen, but at the things which are not seen; for the things which are seen are temporal, but the things which are not seen are eternal."

2 Corinthians 5:7 ". . . for we walk by faith, not by sight."

Ephesians 6:16 ". . . in addition to all, taking up the shield of faith with which you will be able to extinguish all the flaming arrows of the evil one."

Hebrews 11:1 "Now faith is the assurance of things hoped for, the conviction of things not seen."

Unconcern vs. Attentiveness

Luke 6:31 "Treat others the same way you want them to treat you."

Philippians 2:3–4 "Do nothing from selfishness or empty conceit, but with humility of mind regard one another as more important than yourselves; do not merely look out for your own personal interests, but also for the interests of others."

Romans 12:10 "Be devoted to one another in brotherly love; give preference to one another in honor."

Underachievement vs. Creativity

Genesis 1:27 "God created man in His own image, in the image of God He created him; male and female He created them."

Proverbs 22:29 "Do you see a man skilled in his work? He will stand before kings; He will not stand before obscure men."

Ephesians 2:10 "For we are His workmanship, created in Christ Jesus for good works, which God prepared beforehand so that we would walk in them."

Colossians 3:23 "Whatever you do, do your work heartily, as for the Lord rather than for men,

1 Peter 4:10 As each one has received a special gift, employ it in serving one another as good stewards of the manifold grace of God."

Unreliability vs. Responsibility

Romans 14:12 "So then each one of us will give an account of himself to God."

Galatians 6:5 "For each one will bear his own load."

Jamess 4:17 "Therefore, to one who knows the right thing to do and does not do it, to him it is sin."

Wastefulness vs. Resourcefulness

Matthew 25:14–26 "For it is just like a man about to go on a journey, who called his own slaves and entrusted his possessions to them.

To one he gave five talents, to another, two, and to another, one, each according to his own ability; and he went on his journey. Immediately the one who had received the five talents went and traded with them, and gained five more talents. In the same manner the one who had received the two talents gained two more. But he who received the one talent went away, and dug a hole in the ground and hid his master's money.

Now after a long time the master of those slaves came and settled accounts with them. The one who had received the five talents came up and brought five more talents, saying, 'Master, you entrusted five talents to me. See, I have gained five more talents.' His master said to him, 'Well done, good and faithful slave. You were faithful with a few things, I will put you in charge of many things; enter into the joy of your master.'

Also the one who had received the two talents came up and said, 'Master, you entrusted two talents to me. See, I have gained two more talents.' His master said to him, 'Well done, good and faithful slave. You were faithful with a few things, I will put you in charge of many things; enter into the joy of your master.'

And the one also who had received the one talent came up and said, 'Master, I knew you to be a hard man, reaping where you did not sow and gathering where you scattered no seed. And I was afraid, and went away and hid your talent in the ground. See, you have what is yours.'

But his master answered and said to him, 'You wicked, lazy slave, you knew that I reap where I did not sow and gather where I scattered no seed.

Then you ought to have put my money in the bank, and on my arrival I would have received my money back with interest.

Therefore take away the talent from him, and give it to the one who has the ten talents. For to everyone who has, more shall be given, and he will have an abundance; but from the one who does not have, even what he does have shall be taken away. Throw out the worthless slave into the outer darkness; in that place there will be weeping and gnashing of teeth.'"

Luke 16:10 "He who is faithful in a very little thing is faithful also in much; and he who is unrighteous in a very little thing is unrighteous also in much."

John 6:12–13 "When they were filled, He said to His disciples, 'Gather up the leftover fragments so that nothing will be lost.' So they gathered them up, and filled twelve baskets with fragments from the five barley loaves which were left over by those who had eaten."

Willfulness vs. Submission

Proverbs 13:13 "The one who despises the word will be in debt to it, but the one who fears the commandment will be rewarded."

Proverbs 13:18 "Poverty and shame will come to him who neglects discipline, but he who regards reproof will be honored."

Proverbs 13:24 "He who withholds his rod hates his son, but he who loves him disciplines him diligently."

Proverbs 15:32 "He who neglects discipline despises himself, but he who listens to reproof acquires understanding."

Ephesians 6:1–3 "Children, obey your parents in the Lord, for this is right. HONOR YOUR FATHER AND MOTHER (which is the first commandment with a promise), SO THAT IT MAY BE WELL WITH YOU, AND THAT YOU MAY LIVE LONG ON THE EARTH."

Titus 3:1 "Remind them to be subject to rulers, to authorities, to be obedient, to be ready for every good deed."

CHARACTER QUALITY DEFINITIONS

Old-Self Character Quality Definitions

Aggravating – tendency to annoy, irritate, stir up strife

Aloofness – state of being without sympathy or desire to associate with others

Anger – a violent feeling excited by a real or supposed wrong often accompanied by the desire for vengeance

Anxiety – painful or apprehensive uneasiness of mind, usually over an impending or anticipated ill

Apathy – dismissal of or reluctance toward a particular idea, person, group, often experienced as a lack of emotion

Bitterness – poisonous anger, even hatred, at the perception of being treated unfairly or because of unmet expectations

Carelessness – immaturity in words, actions, attitudes; exhibiting a lack of forethought or thoroughness

Complaining – expressing dissatisfaction, pain, resentment; finding fault

Contentiousness – actions or speech that is likely to cause people to argue or disagree

Covetousness – strong desire for that which belongs to another; greed

Cruelty – willful or knowing causing of pain, torment, or distress to others, often finding pleasure in it

Deception – act of misleading or causing others to believe what is false or disbelieve what is true

Discouragement –feeling of having lost hope or confidence

Disorganization – disorder; the lack of orderly arrangement

Disrespect – attitude of heart that leads people to treat God and others in ways that demonstrate lack of esteem, favor, honor, value, appreciation

Double-mindedness – state of being restless, confused, unstable, uncertain in thoughts, actions, behaviors

Extravagance – lack of restraint in spending money or using resources

Fearfulness – dread or apprehension brought about by an expectation of evil, danger, rejection, obstacles, or consequences; timidity

Foolishness – void of understanding or sound judgment; action taken without regard to the divine law and glory or to one's own eternal happiness

Harshness – quality of being unpleasant, rough, severe in words or actions

Haste – quickness of action without thinking carefully about what will happen as a result

Hypocrisy – act of professing belief in something but behaving in a way that is contrary to that belief; looking down on others when we ourselves are flawed

Impurity – immorality in thought or deed; wickedness

Inconsistency – quality of not always acting or behaving in the same way

Indifference – lack of interest or concern

Judgment – condemnation; taking the place of God in making a determination about someone's motives or eternal salvation and purposes

Laziness – lack of effort

Prejudice – an adverse opinion or leaning formed without just grounds or before having sufficient knowledge

Pride – unreasonable conceit in one's own superiority in talents, beauty, wealth, or accomplishments, manifesting as a lofty attitude, distance, and often contempt of others

Resistance – act of standing against, opposing, being unwilling to yield

Restlessness – state of being unhappy about a situation and desiring change to the point that one is uneasy or disturbed

Rudeness – failure to have or show concern or respect for the rights and feelings of other people

Self-centeredness – concern solely for one's own needs, desires, or interests

Self-indulgence – habit of feeding the passions of the flesh, indulging ourselves in any pleasure that is harmful to our souls and does not spring from faith

Selfishness – concern exclusively or excessively with oneself, seeking or concentrating on one's own advantage, pleasure, or well-being without regard to others

Self-pity – state of feeling sorry for oneself, especially in an exaggerated or self-indulgent manner

Stinginess – state of being unwilling to give, spend, or share possessions or money

Tearing down – criticizing; expressing harsh judgment

Unawareness – state of acting without thought, inattentive, or ignorant of what is going on around you

Unbelief – disbelief in divine revelation; doubt, either obstinate and hard-hearted or with a sincere desire to believe

Unconcern – state of having or showing no interest

Underachievement – state of not doing as well as one is capable of doing

Unreliability – quality of being unable to be depended upon

Wastefulness – act of failing or neglecting to use that which is potentially useful

Willfulness – refusal to yield to authority

New-Self Character Quality Definitions

Alertness – being aware of that which is taking place around me so I can have the right response to it

Attentiveness – showing the worth of a person by giving him undivided attention, and showing respect and courtesy

Availability – making my own schedule and priorities secondary to the wishes of God and those I am serving

Boldness – willingness to venture out and do the right thing at the right time regardless of obstacles or fears I may face

Caution – knowing how important right timing is in accomplishing right actions

Compassion – conveying deep love and concern and meeting the needs of those facing struggles and distress

Contentment – realizing that in Christ I have all I need

Creativity – being resourceful and imaginative in using the best of the goods and talents I have to serve the Lord

Decisiveness – the ability to finalize difficult decisions based on accurate facts, wise counsel, and clear direction from God's Word

Deference – limiting my freedom in order not to offend the tastes of those whom God has called me to serve

Determination – purposing to accomplish God's goals in God's time regardless of the opposition

Diligence – regarding each task as a special assignment from the Lord and using all my energies to accomplish it

Discernment – the God-given ability to recognize the difference between truth and error, between good and evil

Discretion – the ability to avoid words, actions, and attitudes which could result in undesirable consequences

Edifying – choosing gracious words that bless, build up, and encourage others

Enthusiasm – being positive, optimistic, and zealous even when I experience setbacks or disappointments

Faith – confidence that actions rooted in God's Word will yield the best outcome even when I can't see how

Faithfulness – fulfilling my commitments to God and others even if it means unexpected sacrifice

Flexibility – not setting my affections on ideas or plans that could be changed by God or others

Forgiveness – clearing the record of those who have wronged me and allowing God to love them through me

Generosity – realizing that all I have belongs to God and using it for His purposes

Gentleness – showing personal care, tenderness, and the love of Christ toward others

Honesty – accurately reporting past facts, present observations, and future intentions

Hospitality – cheerfully sharing food, shelter, spiritual refreshment, and myself with those whom God brings into my life

Humility – recognizing that my achievements result from the investments of others in my life

Integrity – being as genuine on the inside as I appear to be on the outside

Joy – expressing delight in my relationship with Christ, His creation, others and my circumstances as I live in harmony with the Lord and others

Kindness – doing good to others from the heart in thought, word, and deed

Love – caring for others without having personal reward as my motive

Obedience – listening to the voice of, submitting to the will of, and following Christ

Orderliness – preparing myself and my surroundings so I will achieve the greatest efficiency

Patience - Enduring troubles, especially those caused by other people, without complaining or retaliating

Peacemaking – seeking, pursuing, and promoting harmony in my relationships

Persuasiveness – gently guiding vital truths around another's mental roadblocks without being insensitive or pushy

Resourcefulness – wise use of that which others would normally overlook or discard

Responsibility – recognizing and doing what God and those in authority over me require

Reverence – Recognizing and honoring the authority of God with awe and fear

Self-control – restraining my emotions and actions when I feel provoked

Submission – quickly and cheerfully carrying out the direction of those who are responsible for me

Thankfulness – expressing appreciation to God and others for ways in which they have benefited my life

Thriftiness – not letting myself or asking others to spend that which is not necessary

Tolerance – acceptance of others as unique creations of God in varying degrees of maturity

Trust – confident rest in God's character, His promises, and His love for me

Virtue – the moral excellence and purity of spirit that radiate from my life as I obey God's Word

Wisdom – seeing and responding to life's situations from God's frame of reference

ACKNOWLEDGMENTS

First and foremost, I give thanks to God who intervened in my life when my eyes and heart were fixed on this earth and it did not even occur to me to look heavenward.

My generous husband, James, you are endlessly supportive of every new adventure I want to take us on—including this one. Thank you! I am forever grateful for your consistent hard work that allowed me to stay home and cultivate godly character in our kids. I appreciate your steady faithfulness to this woman who is pretty much unrecognizable as the young girl you married so many years ago.

My amazing kids, Ian and Adrianna, you continually enrich our lives in infinite ways, and you gave me a reason to write this book. I am so grateful God chose me to be your mom! Watching you grow and mature into such amazing human beings brings me tremendous joy. Haley, we are beyond blessed to have you in this category now too. I love you guys so much!

To so many sisters in Christ who have faithfully prayed for me and my family, discipled me, nurtured my intimacy with Christ, encouraged me, pushed me out of my comfort zone, kept me accountable: my mom, Sue, my sister, Melissa, my sister-in-law, Tracy, as well as Julie, Heather, Kary, Michelle, and Cara; the Best Small Group Ever—Deb,

Vicki, Jenny, Cheryl, Britt, Amy, Misty, and Denise; my Faithful Friends prayer group—Jennifer, Ann, Rebecca, Laura, and Connie. I am blessed beyond measure to have each one of you in my life!

To the humble men whose teaching I have been so blessed to sit under: Pastor Gary, Pastor Paul, and Pastor Jake. You have challenged me not to trust your words, but to study God's Word for myself. Each of you has promoted my growth in unique ways and encouraged and equipped me to live out my faith. Without the solid foundation your teaching has provided, I doubt I would have had the courage for this venture. Thank you!

I love you all and am so grateful for you!

Thank You for Reading
Off with the Old, On with the New!

I truly appreciate all of your feedback, and your input will make the next version of this book and any future books better.

Please take two minutes now to leave a review on Amazon letting me know what you thought of the book.

Thanks so much!
—Stephanie Ripple

www.ingramcontent.com/pod-product-compliance
Lightning Source LLC
Chambersburg PA
CBHW071755120626
46550CB00002B/798